P9-AFD-055

CHINESE ARCHITECTURE

CHINESE

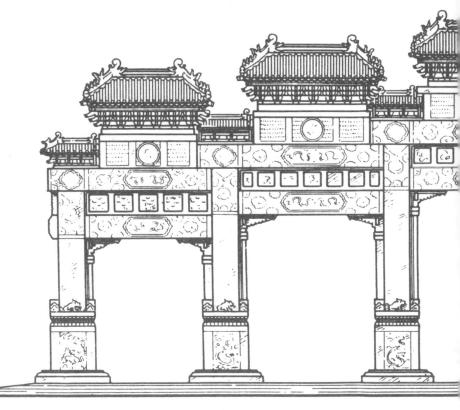

ARCHITECTURE

Poems by Aleda Shirley

THE UNIVERSITY OF GEORGIA PRESS

ATHENS AND LONDON

© 1986 by Aleda Shirley
Published by the University of Georgia Press
Athens, Georgia 30602

Designed by Betty P. McDaniel
Set in 10 on 13 Linotron 202 Meridien
The paper in this book meets the guidelines for
permanence and durability of the Committee on
Production Guidelines for Book Longevity of the
Council on Library Resources.

Printed in the United States of America

90 89 88 87 86   5 4 3 2 1

Library of Congress Cataloging in Publication Data

√ Shirley, Aleda.
Chinese architecture.

I. Title.
PS3569.H557C4 1986   811'.54   86-4283
ISBN 0-8203-0870-6 (alk. paper)
ISBN 0-8203-0871-4 (pbk.: alk. paper)

FOR MICHAEL MCBRIDE

The publication of this book is supported by a grant from the National Endowment for the Arts, a federal agency.

ACKNOWLEDGMENTS

The author and publisher gratefully acknowledge the following publications where these poems first appeared.

American Poetry Review: "The Rivers Where They Touch," "A Hundred Circles"

American Voice: "Small Talk"

Chelsea: "Bull's Eye," "Talking in Bed"

Denver Quarterly: "Speculations on the Pearl"

Georgia Review: "Chinese Architecture," "The Subject Is *You Understood*"

Indiana Review: "My Parents When They Were Young"

Louisville Review: "On Rising"

Mississippi Review: "One Summer Night," "Dreams of You Come in Pairs"

Poetry: "One of a Number of Good Intentions," "The Feel of Not to Feel It," "Tertium Quid," "The Wandering Year," "Finding the Room," "Sunset Grand Couturier," "L'Ivresse des Grandes Profondeurs"

Poetry Northwest: "Reasons for Flight," "Idiot Savant," "Let Me Tell You How It Happened"

Prairie Schooner: "I Will Give You Three Seasons" and "Voices Inside Voices," reprinted by permission of University of Nebraska Press. Copyright 1986 University of Nebraska Press.

Shenandoah: "Detail of a Portrait of a Man Reading a Volume of James," copyright 1980 by Washington and Lee University. "Béance," copyright 1982 by Washington and Lee University. "The Book of the Ocean to Cynthia," copyright 1983 by Washington and Lee University. All reprinted with the permission of the Editor.

Tar River Poetry: "Still Life," "Moving Around Time"

Tendril: "Alchemies"

Virginia Quarterly Review: "Magical Thinking," "Open Ending," "Because of the Rose," "Hostage to Fortune"

"One Summer Night" appeared in the 1985 edition of the *Anthology of Magazine Verse and Yearbook of American Poetry.*

The author is also grateful to the Kentucky Arts Council for a grant that allowed her to complete this book.

CONTENTS

ONE

The Rivers Where They Touch   3
The Wandering Year   5
The Feel of Not to Feel It   7
One of a Number of Good Intentions   9
Tertium Quid   11
Speculations on the Pearl   13
White Birds   15
Sunset Grand Couturier   17
Béance   19
L'Ivresse des Grandes Profondeurs   21
One Summer Night   23
Because of the Rose   25
My Parents When They Were Young   27
Still Life   29
Small Talk   30
Talking in Bed   32
Driving Away in the Rain, the Changing Light   34
Voices Inside Voices   36
The Way Back   38
Detail of a Portrait of a Man Reading a Volume of James   40

TWO

Chinese Architecture   45
A Hundred Circles   47
Let Me Tell You How It Happened   48
Open Ending   50
Idiot Savant   51

Bull's Eye   53

August Curving   55

Magical Thinking   56

Moving Around Time   58

Hostage to Fortune   59

Alchemies   61

The Subject Is *You Understood*   62

On Rising   64

This World and This One   65

I Will Give You Three Seasons   67

Finding the Room   69

Reasons for Flight   71

Dreams of You Come in Pairs   73

The Book of the Ocean to Cynthia   75

Even from the simplest, the most realistic point of view, the countries which we long for occupy, at any given moment, a far larger place in our actual life than the country in which we happen to be.

Proust, *Swann's Way*

ONE

THE RIVERS WHERE THEY TOUCH

At the confluence of the Amazon and the Rio Negro
the blue water of one and the black water
of the other run in separate stripes for ten miles.
The seam shimmers like a thin line of music
and stuns the pilot, passing over.
Through binoculars, he sees the wet spine
of the pink dolphin who, rising from the water
on moonless nights, assumes a man's form
and roams the river towns in search of love.
Maybe it is through this passage,
where fish from both rivers feed
on rich clotted algae, that the dolphin

must flow before he takes his human shape.
It's not difficult to imagine what the pilot
sees: one river seeming always to sleep
as the other slides past, toward the Atlantic
where it stains the water with silt
for a hundred miles. Nor is it hard to imagine
the Frenchman who first mapped these waters
and discovered, by accident, that the planet bulged
at the equator. As perfection cracked ·
like rotting mahogany around him, he must have seen
the river holding drowned faces the way the sky
held stars before any man ever looked up at it.

Vines wrap the jacaranda and coil around the moon:
not one ray of its stolen light escapes. The stars,
tucked in the wings of a thousand toucans,
crackle air so hot and black it seems
sifted through narcosis. Falling backwards

from his boat, the diver would see,
beneath the surface busy with leaves and eels,
how the rivers don't seem separate after all
and perhaps tell us what night so often tells
the pilot, the cartographer, the pair of lovers
sighing from a bridge: that an edge
is never a simple or a sudden thing.

THE WANDERING YEAR

Last August I looked out the window by your bed
and thought, for a moment, the silver maple
in the neighbors' yard was full
of tropical birds, green
and green-gold, breathing in unison.

In October the maple stretched into the room
and traced thin gold branches
on the quilt. A brittle leaf moved
along the sill and the seeds of the pomegranate
we split for breakfast

were garnets you dripped across my thighs
and strung onto the strands of light.
The sky, in January, was so smooth a child
could have skated on it. You walked
under that sky, a bag of birdseed in your arms,

snow glinting like age in your beard.
For the first time I saw that
the silver maple was truly silver,
its limbs bare, its bark
sleek with ice. Even if I stayed still a long time,

I knew that the planet would steadily circle
the sun, and the seasons catch up
with me, one way or another.
The ancient Egyptians counted 365 days, exactly;
over the centuries,

their year wandered, each month occurring
in a different season. But this is spring:
the ground thaws and loses
its pavé brilliance.
The tulips you arrange in a black bowl

on the table are no less stunning
than if they flared from the lunar seas.
Beside the forsythia, the gingko is pinching
off bits of March or April sun, salting
them away for fall.

THE FEEL OF NOT TO FEEL IT

The rent goes up each August, paint peels
in spirals from the bathroom ceiling, neighbors
graduate or marry, move on, and still, when someone
suggests an airy efficiency on a quieter street,
I scurry to check the kettle, change the record,
the subject. It's not that I like it here
particularly or that I'm hiding anything; things
are just simpler this way. When close friends
talk of secret clubhouses, old boyfriends, the night
their senior class got suspended for spiking
the punch with grain alcohol, I think
of Buffalo Gap, York County, Don Bonafacio

and when people I'm introduced to ask me
where I'm from I say here. Ten years: it's taken me
that long not to think of the gradual precision
of monsoon, rain coming earlier each morning
until it's constant for a month, my disappointment
when a Braniff pilot announced we were passing
over the equator and I looked down, the gray pony
stabled near the James, of the romance a word
like *home* held for me, the exotic syllables
of mortgage. Ten years is a long time:

my first lover left because I wouldn't move,
another told me adolescence was a stifling room
I'd never left. He was probably right: even now,
aroused, I sometimes smell sampaguita, soy sauce,
the red wax the houseboy rubbed on the floors
with a coconut shell. Yes, it's painful,
but no more so than the alternative, all the luggage

I'd have to transfer from port to port.
At my familiar window I've discovered
clichés everyone seems to know, that morning
is an old lie we believe again and again, that honesty
sometimes can't help but be circumstantial. There are days
the river is a dirty turquoise, days it's silver
and remarkable in the rain. I needn't remark it,
not any more, having seen it that way before.

ONE OF A NUMBER OF GOOD INTENTIONS

Consider that if you'd listened for years, peered
at the stray fact left ajar long ago until it grew
transparent, secrets might lose their allure
and you would find yourself yearning for a shallow
set of facts about something complex. How,
on winter afternoons at the museum, the parquet floor
and oval of sky would intrigue you more
than the paintings with their allegorical significance.
Since you would be unable to find a word
scraped clean of connotation, what comfort
you would take from opera, passionately sung
in a language you don't know. Other times
you would be moved to tears by an empty pause,
two cranial hands that asked nothing of you.

Though unlikely, it is possible someone
might try to speak to you, say *tree*
and mean your tree, the willow, the day
you hid under its pale skirt as adult voices
shook all the windowpanes in the house.
Say *cat* and mean the Manx that belonged
to the first woman you loved, the August evenings
on an apartment fire escape. Or perhaps
someone would whisper *time* and mean
your mother's gold wristwatch, its crystal
cloudy from wear, the perfume around her:
kid gloves, cigarettes, the tangerine peels
on the front seat of her green Oldsmobile.

I, too, would try. Hoping that then I might
say *love* and mean mine, for you, for whatever

would remain after I'd dipped a white cloth
in ammonia and wiped from the framed glass
dust, images, memories; mine,
for whatever's utter, whatever's left.

TERTIUM QUID

Silence is a virgin by default:
no one asked. So much a part of the landscape
of night or nature we don't notice
her absence or presence until much later,
the way I see her now, a summer
too late. She stood between us
in clothes shimmering or matte, the surface
more striking than the color.
She might have been trying to warn us
of her trickiness, how like the moon's
is her vanity, her solitude.
Remember? We watched her comb her hair,
admired her immaculate scalp. And never guessed
she was hiding her bad side in the dark,
night after night.

            Now she's turned full-face
and we see the thin scar on her cheek,
an uneven hairline. Yet how lovely she is
now that she's stopped arranging her features
for the camera. Perhaps her manner of arrival—
always unexpected, just when you've given up
hope—accounts for her spacious promise,
her credibility. She stirs
her coffee or bends to lace up her shoes,
moves through generality with the ease
of a woman moving through an ordinary morning.
It's possible the phone will ring with bad news,
that she will grow bored by the tedium
of tables and children's voices.

But it's just as likely she will
take into her long arms what comes
of a girl's flute through an open window. That we,
apprehending this for the first time, will reach
across a barrier dense as memory
and in touching her, at whatever angle
we find her face bent, touch each other.

SPECULATIONS ON THE PEARL

In 1917, May C. Plant and the jeweler Cartier struck a deal:
her Fifth Avenue mansion
for two strands of pearls.
Forty years later, the pearls were sold for $150,000,
the house worth millions.

*

I imagine her dark-eyed,
with slow, pale shoulders. Something—a phrase of music,
the last word of an intimate
whisper—caught in her throat, fluttering there.
And though she had drawn the pearls across her arms
and dangled them
in the clattery wafers of city sunlight,
she did not try them on
until the papers were signed and witnessed,
the lawyers out the door,
until every trace of her old life was cleared from the house.
Opening her closet
she stroked the options hanging there and chose
ice-pink silk, a simple neckline.

*

Still, why did she want them so?
They came dearly.
I know she was much-adored
but was there a secret, something to do with the sea,
in her past?
Was a boy she couldn't forget drowned in the Atlantic
off Newport—and the pearls, each of them, evocative
of his tongue across her clavicle,

his tongue at the nape of her neck?
Her breath grew shallow. She fastened the emerald clasp.

*

Maybe the trade had nothing to do with regret.
Maybe she was lovely, aging,
superstitious, and this was a way to wear
time, wear distance.
Two thousand years before, a Persian empress
had worn such a necklace in her winter palace.
Was she signalling chasteness to God?
A French king had sipped on ground pearls, believing
they could rid him of madness,
restore his virility.

*

Cut-glass, parquet, the crush of silk and sable:
dinner is served.
Are the candles flickering?—it is the guests, aghast.
Aloof, adorned, she enters the hall.

WHITE BIRDS

We speak of wings beating and fluttering, of engines
turning over as they ignite, yet
the motion of flight is smooth. If
I reached inside your skull, would I touch
a globe with the world drawn on it?
or something crackling, the pages
of a letter carried away by the wind
to the yard's brownest corner? I find evidence of winter

everywhere: the skyscrapers hide their shadows;
the skaters turn white, flare,
and disappear. The goldfish who swam inside the moon
last summer are motionless.
So are the barges on the river.
I think of the day we drove through the flat fields
of the Eastern Shore where gulls gathered by the hundreds
and long for you

as though you were sailing the lost river old sailors
claim runs through the Chesapeake Bay.
If the stars weren't weighting the night down,
it would slap against the window.
If the house moved, it would leave a wake.
I am trying to sleep and clear
my mind as one clears a mirror by moving away.
When I close my eyes I see a river so thin

one navigates it like a tightrope stretched
over mist; I see the confluence of our sky
with that of another planet,
three or four moons gleaming there. Morning

will reveal salt-lines on the walls that tell me
someone has been here, and left, and will return.
The carp will thaw. Standing before the mirror I'll see
a line of birds, some portion of your face.

SUNSET GRAND COUTURIER

You've called to say you're on your way;
I'm outside, picking zinnias for the table. The children
two houses down shoot
free throws and the ball
sounds like slow, steady applause for the mild evening,
the possibilities in the blue air.
Wittgenstein imagined someone pointing to a place
in the iris of a Rembrandt
and saying, 'The walls in my room should be painted
this color.' And why not?
What if I scooped up the air around me and demanded
a dress the color of dusk?
Would that be vanity?
I am wearing such a dress,
for you. The threads that glint in the weave
are fireflies flickering in the apple branches;

the sheen on the collar the bells at Vespers
from the church on Peterson Hill;
the splotches of scarlet along the hem
the first sumac hedging the sky.
Does the dress mean I want you to pass
your wrists completely
through me, deeper
than the choir of tongues, the many hands,
that have touched me in the past? to merge
with no seam, like water into water, daylight
into dusk? Or, more simply, is it
a desire for that union
each of us loses
in the first months of life

when the soft sunlight on our cheeks
and mother and milk are one thing? Imagine:

mourning doves, as they begin to grieve,
can fly right through me
and, in bones suddenly hollow,
I feel the urge
to go south, the urge to return.
If rain falls, I can pass into the yellow window
flaring on a dark street
and find you
sitting in a corner chair, the candlelight
bouncing inside hurricane globes.
You touch my hair with warm dry hands
and my dress turns the color
of a cello, seasoned
for years in Italian sunlight,
of the room behind the half-open door
the girl in the painting peered through.

BÉANCE

In her narrow house she, nervous and alert, dreams
of magnolia blossoms, huge fleshy leaves filling
the room. She wakes beside him. Past and present
converge: an animal with white pointed teeth
crawls out of his crotch. She smoothes its fur, eggs
it on as it stares at her implacably as ice.

From journeys to Singapore, the desert, the polar ice
cap, he brings gifts: an abacus, a portrait of a dreamy
girl said to resemble her, an enamel box. Marble eggs
from Bangkok knob the pockets of his coat and fill
the flat sky at his departure. His blue cap, tooth-
brush, razor, are gone. She touches one by one the presents

he left, clicks the abacus, feels suddenly a wet presence
curling like a bat in her belly. Aspirin and iced
tea don't calm her; sensitive to cold, her teeth
ache, temples throb. Infants bald as moons dream
her fate—but fate is too large a word for what fills
her small apartment, her gnawed ovaries. Egg

and sperm, shouldn't there be a click, a snap, when egg
and sperm collide? There is only her mother presenting
the baby with a silver cup, a brisk doctor who fills
her first with relief, his hands cool as chrome or ice,
then dread, as he tells her that the bad dreams
are a normal reaction. A pause. A brief smile, even teeth:

"I can't deliver anything." Later, brushing her teeth,
she spreads out lips thick as a llama's and, like egg-
shell, her skin is pale and brittle. She dreamed .

19

of mirrors the night before, a duffel bag spilling presents,
of candlelight, clean linen, champagne on ice.
On cue, he arrives with a flourish, a peacoat filled

with jade chessmen, silk scarves. *I've had my fill,*
she whispers. When he touches her she grits her teeth
and wonders if one is born with a glass jaw and ice
for blood, born loving regret. *Spilt milk, counted eggs,*
you mustn't cry, her mother had said. *Always present*
your best face to the world. It's only a dream.

L'IVRESSE DES
GRANDES PROFONDEURS

For a while, the colors distracted her from thought
of home; at a depth of fifteen feet, red
turned pink; further on it was black,
then disappeared. That first winter she killed
time counting the sheets and table linens,
designing a centerpiece of shells.
Our noticing them is what puts things in a room
and her rearrangements pleased him; he saw what
surrounded him for the first time in years.
The air tasted like pennies. She swallowed hard
as she realized love had only so many fingers:
his, on all the buttons down the back
of her dress. Looking up she saw footsteps, rings
in the trees, rows of windows brimming
with other people's secrets. Once these things
would have meant possibility, brochures
of desire fluttering toward her. Now,
drunk with the rapture of the great depths,
she's forgotten sunlight and goodbye are
options; at any given moment she feels unaccountably
lucky, as someone might on a day the first
characteristic weather of a season breaks through
and one red convertible after another passes
by on the freeway. Night is the destination
that lures her, ambience the one element in which
she feels at home. Snow falls on the outside
of the year and the lens of the sky, gritty
with North African sand and volcanic dust, reddens
the moon. She senses the invisible lips
that would appear if she powdered a pane from one

of those yellow windows. Yet how can she call
this suffering? She is at home. The dark fills up
with invitations. Deception matters
less and less as she learns the difference
between it and truth: lying requires a reason.
His is to have her with him, to grow inured
to her presence. She desires to be touched,
on all sides at the same time.

ONE SUMMER NIGHT

The sherbet-colored lawn chairs arranged
themselves in pairs, like dancers,
and my grandfather rattled his newspaper,
cigarette smoke curling like a bad mood around him.
This was how it was twenty years ago
in Oakland, Kentucky: my uncles telling jokes
as they took turns turning the ice cream freezer,
my grandmother drying her hands on her apron
and, there, by the door, my mother talking softly
to her sisters about a time longer ago than this one
I long for. Slow, like a slow dance:
my cousins and I waded through green shadows
and touched the tips of honeysuckle
to the tips of our tongues. The walnut,
heavy with fruit, was a ship with tall pink sails,
the patio a kind of shore and the adults calling
Girls, ice cream the light of a lighthouse
beaming across dark distance. Night fell
gently as if it were bending down to look
in our faces; waving sparklers
we filled the air with rhinestones, so profuse
and lovely they had to be fake.

Odd now to think no one had walked
on that moon rising in the mimosa's shallow limbs
and odd to understand how, more than that night, I want
to know they want it back as much as I do. For this
I would forfeit my dozen cities, even the loveliest one;
the thin clear goodnight the child calls
from across the street; my lover's hands
on my upper arms as he rises above me in the dark.

I'd give up the secrets I've coaxed from memory's
closed fist and the ability to articulate them.
Though not the desire.

BECAUSE OF THE ROSE

When he left, my father asked us what we wanted.
My sisters wanted dresses, lace, ribbons.
I asked for a spool
of thread so fine it turned silver in the rain,
or a rose that would open and, when
the petals fell, feel like time on my hands.
The gift had a price. I was taken far
away to a house hedged with roses. For days
the scent sickened
me: too sweet, too full
of the future. I arranged ivy in a vase
and folded my soft sashes. I watched
in my square mirror events
in another part of the world:

there was my father at the edge of a field;
he might have been weeping
or looking for rain in the sky. And, there, my sisters
calling their children; my brother sailing
home, schools of perch swimming through his face.
The man of the house was inscrutable.
One morning I found a yellow scarf
at the foot of my bed,
a bar of sunlight. I saw him
only in shadows, after supper. He smelled
of the wind. He asked me never to leave.
His hands in a pair of dove-gray gloves touched
the moon in a window,
then touched my face. He let me go,

but with conditions: I had seven days.
And what days! On the seventh morning,
I heard my sisters' bright chatter,
my nephews stirring from their beds,
my father whistling on the porch.
I found a bunch of violets
left by a boy with rough hands.
Later, I would understand how love often takes
the form of a promise almost broken
and that what happened happened because,
instead of a gift, I asked for a symbol.
We married: one of us
had changed. Now I have a child and in my garden
the memory of a dozen summers.

MY PARENTS WHEN THEY
WERE YOUNG

Sleet whips the trees against the house
and pushes clouds across the sky. Or maybe
it's the sky moving behind clouds:
for that's the way I've begun to feel age,
something absolute shifting behind days
of sunlight, days of snow.
Snug in its brown skin, the turkey
smells of sage; the cranberry sauce glimmers
like a big fake jewel in the revere bowl.
And my father, leaning
against the gray window, muses how
when I was seven, he was the age I am now;
my mother tips forward in her rocker and asks
if I remember them when they were young.

And I try to erase the definition
of smile and frown in her face,
to pluck out the salt strands
in his salt-and-pepper hair, to remember
when they were the grown-ups and late at night
was a place they went without me:
if I could see them walking, hand in hand,
around the square in Murfreesboro
as dusk trembled on their shoulders
and the courthouse crept off into darkness
and the movie marquee lit up . . . but I am a child,
insinuating myself into this scene,
crying, from a sitter's porch,
Come back, come back.

They are asking me to remember
because they are afraid of dying.
I want to whisper: I know, I know—
you read me a story and I fought sleep,
I wanted the tale to go on forever;
you carried me in from the car
in the middle of the night and went back out
in the rain to get my doll or the moon,
whatever it was I'd left on the backseat.
Do I tell them how some physicists believe
that on the subatomic level time may move
in both directions? Only the sea can remember
everywhere it's been, and we'll have
between us always those twenty-odd years.

STILL LIFE

FOR EMMA APRILE

The child stands by the window and brushes
her hair. Snow has turned all the roofs
in the neighborhood white and filled her room
with a pale porous light. For the first time
she has imagined telling a secret to a boy
with soft eyes and her hair snaps with static.
Once she heard her mother explain
what hydroplaning was, how between
the car's tires and the pavement was a thin
oily layer of air. This is how she's felt lately:
as though any sudden turn or unplanned stop
could send her crashing into the bare trees
along the parkway or head over heels down
twelve familiar steps to the front hall.

A toddler napping on a pallet in the sunroom,
the winner of the school science fair,
the birthday girl crying over a lost locket—
in her mind these distant selves form
a chain dimmer than the night-light
she still switches on before she goes to bed.
It makes no sense that the world should seem
so fragile just as she is getting taller:
she knows the strength it takes to outgrow
jeans and tennis shoes, to tell the boy who teases her
in homeroom to bug off. And yet, plaiting
her thick gold hair, she feels she's holding the day
in her hands and worries that it might, with no warning,
fall apart like wet paper and float away.

SMALL TALK

The house you grew up in, the diamond
where you played baseball, the front porch where you
first kissed a girl—you show me these things
and ask to see some place I've lived, any
place, a window in a white frame house
that was mine, a tree I might have climbed

as a child. We drive through the park, over
the bridge you've driven across every day
of your life and dusk falls so fast that for a moment
I think it's rain. In bed when the lights
are off and one of us can't sleep, you whisper
show me and I touch myself and remember an ice storm

in the south, school cancelled for a week, mugs
of tomato soup. I touch your leg with mine
and think of the woman who slept away
all the summers of my childhood, the woman who died
when I was a baby and left me alone
with the man who made maps and followed weather

from continent to continent. If only we could
choose our parents: I would have chosen
the one who gardened on weekends and looked after
his invalid wife, rubbing the blue veins
in her wrist with a cool cloth. I heard him
singing, late at night. *Like this,* I tell you

and feel your breath on my hair, two fingers
running down my spine; I remember poison ivy
growing up the chimney, and white iris—

there must have been a garden. If only we could
choose our gifts: I would have done better
than folding the paper sailboat on the gray rug,

covering my face with your hands, and offered
something glittering, like what you showed me: the moon
following the curve of the bridge into another state.

TALKING IN BED

The sky in Manila was green.
Boys squatted in front of the sari-sari stores
and leered. The week before Easter
we watched a flagellant
swing a glass-embedded paddle into his back.
My mother gave a child a balloon and a handful
of centavos. As we rounded the corner I heard
the din: a gang of boys pounced on him and the balloon,
a red one, floated away.

            Dust rose
from the barrio streets and the humidity
was so thick it could have rained and no one
would have noticed. My hair frizzed; I was tired
and wanted to go home. My parents thought
of this day as an opportunity, a marvelous one.
And you, when I described it years later,
pushed back the sheet as if it were
the moonlight that fell across us,
lit a cigarette, and started talking

about the problems of the Third World, what ridiculous
figures Americans cut abroad, and how
shopkeepers must have laughed, behind
our backs, as we bargained
for the mother-of-pearl wind chimes
and monkeypod bowls. It wasn't that I disagreed
with you: I knew even then that the houseboy's pliant
smile concealed contempt. But I was telling
you something else, about trying to sleep

as jeepneys of guards patrolled the compound
and I heard the click of their M16's. One night
crickets blackened the blue tiles of the bathtub; Jesu
vacuumed them up by the hundreds while,
out the window, bats flew in and out
of the streetlight's circle. At Thousand Islands
I cut my foot on a piece of coral.
A staph infection followed: weeks on antibiotics.
I lost my favorite bracelet in a hotel at Baguio
and remember my mother pulling out her opera pumps,
silver with mildew.

           That was all
I was trying to tell you: that I had trouble
sleeping and the sky, in Manila, was green.

DRIVING AWAY IN THE RAIN,
THE CHANGING LIGHT

When I first felt desire, it was nothing
more than the river in the spring flooding
the city with blue
and gold light. The man I loved slept with
his arms folded across his chest.
I never knew what he was protecting.
There were pastels, most of them
nudes, on his walls and in the morning,
half-asleep, I imagined they swam
through light, that those weren't leaves beyond
the window, but algae
and I could have a dress
of blue lace and a filmy shawl. As he slept,
I thought of the submarine river in the Pacific,
said to course faster than any river on land.
How can you tell when one body

of water becomes another? The oceanographers
must know, and those who paint water,
and the cellists. One night
I wanted to walk in the rain,
but he said no, he was tired,
it was too late. So I went alone, wearing
only his shirt. I knew what was coming:
he unfolded his arms and pinched out the flames
at the tips of my breasts. Nothing's
sudden, though nothing, were it a mood
or weather, would come suddenly:
a windstorm the weathermen failed to predict,
a chemical imbalance

in the brain that causes someone to sleep
all day and cry all night. I wept into the circle
of the steering wheel, having forgotten

how careless autumn is with its wealth:
getting in the car, I'd found a leaf, arthritic
with color, and picked it up carefully,
as if it were the hand of someone
older or younger than I. I knew that, with winter,
the river would throw silver shadows across the city
and the sky lower until it felt like the brim
of a gray fedora, a size too small, softened by time.

VOICES INSIDE VOICES

A cold night in February: dusk
hung like cobwebs from the trees.
Had I been an alto I would have pulled
from my sleeve a brown and silver
flower and brushed it past my throat
where it would have stung, like sleet
by the ocean. Instead I took a deep breath;
the goodbye I whispered was not my own;
your mother said it long ago and you,
holding a Chinese kite in one hand

and your grandfather's fist in the other,
said it back. Letting the kite go
you thrust your hand toward
the plane's curved silver door as though
the door might feel your desire and open up
like a mind changing itself. As long
as her face smiled through the porthole
you hoped she'd think better of leaving
but when the plane took off you saw
a big glass sled shattering

as it reached the bottom of the hill.
Yes, I loved you, but that wasn't enough
for either of us. Your gifts—
the turquoise scarf, the striped umbrella,
the ginger jar with its crane motif—no longer
give me pause; they've joined the clutter
of objects I wear or dust. There
was a time I wanted to gather up great
gobs of dusk, stuff it around the base
of a dried arrangement, the way a florist

uses Spanish moss, and send it to you.
Lately, though, when I meet someone
who has the same name as you
and hear in his voice your hello, I can
blow it out as easily as a match.

THE WAY BACK

When I say the word *past* over and over to myself until
it's abstract, almost nonsensical,
sometimes I see a road, lined with cottonwoods,
fields where cattle graze,
and a pond rimmed with red clay.
Then a shimmer, as of rain,
an old rowboat by the pond,
a clump of black-eyed susans, their centers
gleaming navy-blue in the wet light. But, this time,
I can't find the lover's secret I've come after:
how to surprise you
even after we've been together for years.
Though it hasn't been years yet
and I'm in a city where the streets
are arranged in a neat grid and, when I look
north, lead only to the river.
The brain can handle
its bright bits and coiled ribbons too many times:
did we see the remarkable sunrise at the beach
in Delaware or the beach in Virginia?
In what seemed like the middle

of the night, I felt your hands on my face
and heard you telling me to look.
The balcony doors were open
and, through the seam formed by the blue plane
of the sea and the blue plane
of the sky, the sun
had burned a thin red line. Had it been coiled
in a ball, it would have fit in my hand.
In the foreground wheeled gulls, stained
mauve by the shadows.

In the background a single silver jet headed east.
I thought of the other meaning
of flight: if I walked
until I came to nothing but water
would I find a pond, jittery and iridescent
with horseflies? or the river at night, moving
more slowly than the barges making their way
south? or would I find
the ocean, polishing birds and planes
in its glassy surface?
I would be back where I started, at any rate.

DETAIL OF A PORTRAIT OF A MAN
READING A VOLUME OF JAMES

FOR JEREMIAH STARLING

Four years, and I've never asked if you were blond or dark
as a boy. A photograph taken ten years ago
answers nothing; you sit in a glass-sided restaurant
in Venice and, because the water and the glass hold the sky,
everything, except the gold rim of your coffee cup,
is silvered to gray. So any portrait of you
would have to be an arrangement, like a Whistler,
of two predominant colors: black and gold perhaps,
or flesh-color and black. Actual incidents arrange
themselves in two colors. Harmony in silver and blue:

an Eastern jet flies through light snow to New York;
you are on board and the twilled seat-cover,
against the snowy window and your charcoal suit,
grays to a painting's backdrop. You drink coffee,
you are reading a paperback copy of *What Maisie Knew.*
A detail of a portrait of a girl is on the cover;
she languidly turns her hair out from her neck,
small chunks of turquoise stud her ears. She is a portrait
within one. Later, at the ticket counter, the title
is underlined by the fold of your dark pocket.

When critics first looked at "Symphony in White No. 1:
The White Girl," they thought it incomplete,
unfinished; only the texture of the rugs seemed detailed.
Perhaps they were right and, outside the canvas, another
   figure
meets the white girl's stare; over Mrs. Leyland's shoulder
bursts the sudden brightness of her peacock dining room.

Perhaps some ordering power—a magnet of light, Urizen's
    compass—
waits beyond the frames of "Old Battersea Bridge" and
"The Falling Rocket" to gather it all up in literal four-color.
It might be after all. And it helps to explain you.

TWO

CHINESE ARCHITECTURE

The pailou is a symbolic gateway
that defines
the entrance to an ideal space.
Even if you choose

to row a boat out on the water
or wade along the shore,
the pailou says,
This is how you enter the lake.

This is how you enter the part of the city
where white jade and peonies are sold.
Here, an emperor is buried
and, here, a field where horses graze.

It is a structure you long for
if you've ever awakened
from a dream about a house
you've never been in,

if, as a child, you tapped for hollow panels
in the cedar closet
or played in the mossy octagon
formed by a stand of spruce.

Now you are entering a garden.
A silver comb gleams
in grass where, a moment ago,
a young girl held out her printed robe

and sang, *I am wearing silk,*
I am wearing clear sky, seashells, words.
I am wearing a lake
and seven white bridges.

A HUNDRED CIRCLES

When I held your head between my hands
I heard the two oceans that clasped
my childhood, the tropical storm
whose lightning strafed the mats on the floor
of my room, the soft slapping of the pond
on my grandfather's farm where
concentric rings snagged gold from the air
and moved in on themselves or out to me,
a child fanning the water with her fingers.
Now I hear in any water the whisper
that water failed to utter, *come home,*
hurry home; I have been stuck in a motion
so constant it's rigid, that point
in a west Texas landscape where

because there are so many miles behind you
and many still ahead, distance
is grainy as sand, and not one tree
or hill mediates the harshness of the horizon.
But curved inside your touch I've found
the pause between two lovely airs,
a lullabye or August rain, that gray
before the rat-tat-tat gold of the zinnias.
You are the still point the mirror
becomes in a busy room, a clarity
absorbing the couple arguing politics
in the corner and the tumblers clinking ice,
or the moon grinding well-oiled gears
as it sets in one sea or another.

LET ME TELL YOU HOW IT HAPPENED

During the one train ride of my childhood
a woman in a green dress gave me a piece
of gum. I've forgotten where we were going
but remember that the *Life* magazine on the seat
beside me showed a gem becoming pure gesture
on an actress's hand. I might say:
this is what really happened. But what
of the red clouds in the west Texas sky?
my sense that the adults had lied, when
they said the sea was on either side of me,
somewhere? That was the year my grandfather
went slowly deaf and because of this,
and the sunset, the woman's dress was violet
and on the cover of the magazine Ed White

walked through space. Recently I spent a day
at the shore; the weather was clear all the way
to Japan and we weighted the checked cloth's
four corners with shells and driftwood, No,
it wasn't the sea at all, but a restaurant
with many windows and a man in a camel's hair coat
who walked in and so immediately knew me
my knees turned to water or cloth drying
from the inside out on summer grass. He took me
to his apartment and, though it was March, hung
glass birds and balsa snowflakes from the ficus.
This is one detail, but it could have been any room
in which there are two chairs and a window.
The ornaments broke the light into needles

on the hardwood floor and I shivered from
the cold of all the Christmases I wished white
when I was small and when, finally, he touched me
the bee stings and scraped knees of childhood
flared again on my body and his mouth, cool
as calomine, kissed each welt. That might have been
the way it happened: I went home with the man
in the camel coat and he showed me a picture
of the ocean. Or perhaps it was someone else,
a man at another table who told me he had seven
brothers and once drove through the town where
I was born. I cannot tell the difference:
at some point, he moved into me the way a skater
blurs into the final spin of a flawless performance.

OPEN ENDING

It begins with shimmering props:
two glasses of liebfraumilch
and the moon or a candle sputters out
and erases the auburn glints
on her head nodding yes. He twirls
the gold bracelet she wears,
touches her for the first time.

Later, in another room, his hands press
like silence over her ears.
Her body retains the feel of his the way
a leather glove, removed, holds
the shape of its wearer.
He dreams of home: how flat
Illinois is, how smooth Lake Michigan
would be, if he could slip across it
on his bike. The miscellany
on the table by the bed shatters
in the light. A bracelet.
His keys. The digital clock.

She repeats his name to herself
until it is only syllables that fall
off of him. There is a mole in the small
of his spine. In two or three days
she'll wake with a cold
and wonder if he, pedaling
across a silver lake, has one too.
A small loss—this is what
she wants. Over and over again.

IDIOT SAVANT

As he finishes each sentence, he smacks
his lips: thorazine
has confused the signals his brain sends his nerves
and only sleep, stilling him, stills
this tic. He cannot read or write;
he cannot think abstractly. What he can do
is sculpt; the drug
has left unaffected his ability to reach
inside his skull and touch
the images there:

the mustang's slender hooves,
the knotted branches of mesquite
and the thin shadows
they trace on the sand, the fat cacti kneeling
in the wind. These
he renders from fistfuls of clay and sells
for hundreds of dollars
in the cool glass galleries
on the edge of the desert. Neurologists,
unable to account for any

of this, speculate that maybe the mind
will never be able to explain
itself; perhaps it is his total blankness
that allows the savant
this one precision. One of the doctors
compares his mind to a mirror,
extending inward
for a thousand miles. I think

of the power of his concentration and what
it might tell us. Who else, anymore,

is capable of such concentration? Some of us,
in love, can hold
one face singly in our minds, but not for long,
not long enough. Another way
to think about love
is as a kind of useless genius:
we locate,
in the lover's body, that graceful
statue our own
stolid forms have always longed to release.

BULL'S EYE

The skulls of cattle came later. Now
she's still young and I want to tell you
how she goes out in the desert at night,
aims her gun at fat Polaris, and pulls.
Because the star is not a surplus grenade,
volatile and forgotten in a dark shed,
or maybe just because her work went well
that afternoon, nothing happens. Only a sound,
like silver stiffening in the air. What,
after all, are the stars to her?

                              And what
was the moon to the man who threw rock
after rock at its reflection in a lake?
A virgin whose spine clinked like cold metal
when he touched her? A handsome woman
whose chase narrowed his dreams to dark corridors?
The blank face of his mother, itself a lamp,
waiting at some window for him to come home?

I know a man who idly tosses broken shells
and beach glass into the Chesapeake,
throws pebbles at a freshly turned field,
the clear night sky. Over Taurus's eye
Aldebaran shines its double light. The painter
imagined dawn on the bed as a gray quilt,
cool and still. I am asking you to lie there,
for a moment, and listen.

                              Why don't we clear out
the rooms, dismantle the furniture under the stars,
learn backwards how it holds books and guests,
how the table by the window distorts the moon
in its patina? It's this urge to take things apart
that pulls and, in its glimmer, connects us.
If we go indoors, the room will be bare
as a dance floor. Exploding buckshot at the stars
is a thought we share here among the clawed feet
and tabletops, the cushions. Nearby,
the ploughed earth moves like water in the moonlight.

AUGUST CURVING

Red leaves fleck the grass near the museum.
I watch the eyelids of the statues
and think of the warm weight
of your hand on my thigh,
your hand on my hand.
I feel like throwing my voice
into the stone throat of a statue,
calling your name from there.
Or crumbling a leaf in my hand and watching
it burst into a blue clear flame.

MAGICAL THINKING

I am sometimes afraid I love each lover
a little less than the one before, and the first one
most of all: the night the phone rang in the dorm
and the parking lot filled up with snow
and he tied his scarf in a soft knot
around my neck is a scene
I can't forget, the story I would tell
if I ever told the truth when someone asked
what I'm thinking as I swallow the evening's
last wine. Even though it was years ago: the winter
the river froze for the first time in a century
and, despite warnings from the weathermen, eager fathers
took their children out to walk across it.

We went too: the sky was a delicate membrane stretched
between silver capillaries. A lost cat, a woman
singing arias from an old convertible,
would have started the bridge swinging, sent
it crashing down into the hard river. As it was,
only a few cars, clumsy in chains, passed
and later at home, though it could have been any one
of a hundred dusks, he stood by the window
and muttered nothing to the street. He threw his voice
into my throat: at odd moments I would find myself
saying *anguish* or *so what?* as though surprise
were a kind of dark cavity nothing filled.

Last winter was mild. The spring's been cold,
record-breaking freezes every night this week,
but bright days: the sun wheeling its sharp edge
like the saw in silent movies that's always on the verge

of splitting the girl in half. Yesterday I thought I saw
the shape of his hands in the sky broken up by trees.
Then a window opened: a child practicing scales.
Out of nowhere I said *cello, redbud, thaw.*

MOVING AROUND TIME

I'd hide morning in the live coals October
deposits in the trees,
in a pond broken off from the sky,
toss it across a field of grain rising to meet
a formation of skydivers
or slide it into that space, thin as a molecule,
between my face and yours when we dance.

I'd roll afternoon up like a beach towel
still heavy with moisture
and camouflage it against the freckles dusted
like pollen on your arm;
I'd fold it along the curve
of a wooden boat sailing the Intracoastal Waterway
from the Grand Strand to Key West.

Night I'd find curled in worn silk at the back
of the closet or sleeping, like violins,
in a stand of spruce in the mountains
and pull it out only when I'm with you
whose hair lights up
any room we're in and gives off the dry heat
of the Carolina dunes, whose breath on my throat
swells like curtains scooped out
by wind or the sheer wattage of the light.

HOSTAGE TO FORTUNE

Often, when you're away on business, I wake
in the middle of the night with something
urgent or whimsical to tell you
and then, the next morning,
can't remember what it was. And sometimes
I bring in your khakis and oxford cloth shirts,
your socks and underwear,
and pile them, still warm from the dryer, on the bed.
I pull a cuff across my arm and watch
static crackle the hair on my wrist.
When I take a shower
steam brings out the ghost of the aftershave
you put on earlier in the day and for a second,
forgetting, I peer out the shower curtain
to see if you're there.

How fragile your plane would seem
if I stood on the beach where I once lived
and watched it fly inland.
When I'm old I would like to have saved something
to give you—the soft shreds
of a turquoise t-shirt we both claimed,
a jar of rain from a long Sunday afternoon
when we sat on the floor and listened
to sides of albums you'd never played,
the stub of a candle we lit in a mountain cabin
as the new year turned . . . —but why wait?
Metal fatigue;
the inexplicable virus;
a stray bullet in the police pursuit:
I need no reason and I have many.

A few days ago, I sat on a bench outside
the Episcopal Church in a small Indiana town
and waited for you. The July heat thickened shadows
and bent the necks of the daylilies;
I couldn't read the hour on the sundial.
And though I knew your gait,
the changing shape of your face
as you break into a smile,
your hands gesturing
as if they might suddenly toss me
a discus of the slippery light,
I held my breath
as though you were a stranger
who would change my life
walking into my life.

I want the sight of you, ankles stained green,
when you come in from cutting the grass,
the taste of you on my hands in the morning;
I will give you what I've hoarded
and, when I'm frightened into doubt, think
of the night I was afraid to climb
the ladder that led to a warehouse roof
and the city's best view
of the fireworks and how you were behind me all the way,
your hands on either side of my knees,
the sound of your voice,
Don't look down,
you can do it. And I did,
emerging shaken and breathless
into the night's splendid fake stars.

ALCHEMIES

Maybe it wasn't greed that destroyed
Midas but simply a failure to account for how
irrevocable are the consequences of desire.
Later, his gold daughter aflame in the garden,
he cried, 'That wasn't what I meant' and
'I didn't know' but, by then, it was too late

just as one who describes himself as falling
in love is already at the end
of that trajectory. And when teams
of oceanographers search for affordable
ways to concentrate the gold finely dispersed
in seawater, they don't think
of what will happen if they find the method
or of their predecessors bent over athanors
on the Rue des Halles and Goldmaker's Lane in Prague.

None of us is likely to ask what can be
put back, what returned to, as we gather and go,
and yet, late at night, after the affair,
we yearn for the process
that would render the loved face mundane
and still the atoms moving in a pattern
that moves us forever.

THE SUBJECT IS *YOU UNDERSTOOD*

In the smoky light of a corner bar you gleamed
like a lifeguard and, as I walked
to the jukebox, asked me if I had the time.
Before I knew it I was whispering to you
about how the curtains threw
lace birds on my shoulders as I dressed
to go out and about the cardinal that died
when it followed the moon into my windshield.
Your voice was as low as the sky when
rain falls on a town across the river
and through the sunroof of your car
a moist leaf fell in my lap;
I heard, from a neighbor's garden, the sound
of daylilies wearing out their color.
Listen, I said, trying to explain,
holding my mouth to your ear.

You have eyes that in the dark detect phosphorus
in the aquarium and the shadow of wings
on my throat. When I was small I collected
fireflies in a jar because it was
one light I could hold and hold onto.
I tell you this because I have
the time and you have hands that move like hours
across my body; there is a sense
of thunder outside each time you walk
through the door; when you pull off
your shirt static crackles around your head
like a halo of wasps. You crawl
so thoroughly inside me it's as though

I'm filled with sky, blue sky out of which
a ton of sunlight falls. And you say, *Tell me
why you played those songs.* Or, *touch me here.*

ON RISING

It is sometimes in the dark that one remembers
the woman who knew where she would die,
and how she saw her booted foot test
the water before she entered, felt
the weight of the stone,
an off-center pregnancy,
in the pocket of her linen jacket.

But dawn once again, again
the familiar light at the familiar window,
an exhausted peace.
The center lost, but round tables
at each elbow, and a silence afterward,
or a cello in the afternoon.

THIS WORLD AND THIS ONE

I read once that when you look at a painting
of a chair, you see a chair. But
when you look at a photograph in which
that painting appears—say, over a mantel
or between two windows—you see
a painting of a chair,
you perceive the flickering quality
of reality once and twice removed.
A summer morning. I'm sitting at the kitchen table,
waiting for you to return with the Sunday papers.
I've put Vivaldi's "Four Seasons"
on the stereo. Beyond the window,
children play croquet on thick green grass.
I am satisfied with the thunk of the mallet
against the wooden ball,
the thought that, at any moment, you'll drive up

and I'll hear, first, the tires crunch gravel
in the driveway. So what causes the hairline crack
in my perfect contentment?
It separates us, and leaves me
with the idea of you, idling the car
at a stop sign down the street.
I need you home now; I want
you to spread plans for the afternoon
like a deck of cards across the table.
I imagine, not happily,
that if I walked in the study
and pulled out every letter filed in the drawer,
each of them would read itself aloud
in the sender's voice;

that the piles of snapshots would be the same, intact,
except for a girl-sized blank,

a buzzing gray space, where I'm supposed to be,
and I would be out of camera range,
off looking for someone else.
What returns me to the present
is the immediate past, this morning:
the cats' high-spirited romp across the hardwood floor,
your face bent so closely over mine
it blurred into the pale amber light filtered
through the matchstick blinds,
the liquid syllable *June*
repeated again and again in the trees;
my conviction, then, that I could let go of the pillow,
of gravity's insistent, interior pull,
and float off into air so high it knew no season;
that you would be there,
right beside me.

I WILL GIVE YOU THREE SEASONS

The old moon has crumbled away, leaving this silver
slit clean as absence. Light is smeared in the water
with such marvelous excess I think
of tulle in a milliner's shop,
the pennies that gather in the bottom
of pocket or purse. I'm ready.
For once, memory is nothing more
than a soft white cloth

with which I polish the present.
Yes, it is a gift: a thin gold bangle,
a branch of eucalyptus,
the blade of neon
that flashes in the corner of a bar.
I'm not distracted by the past, all done up
in spangles and rain: I could rub
the Ohio all the way to Pittsburgh. I won't deny

someone hurt me once. I could call it a sliver
of ice stuck in the throat.
A sip of brine. I could call it betrayal
and count and re-count the shards
of mirror I broke in anger,
gleaming now in dusty silk thrown
in the back of the closet because he said
I looked good in red. But my wrist pulses

with nothing more than the strip of skin
my watch hid from the sun
and the river floats its lights into the bridge
which arches, like a skydiver, over it.

Summer hides inside every season
in much the way an unlit lamp waits in a dark room,
the way I sleep in your arms
as you read late into the night.

FINDING THE ROOM

For months I would wake you up
and tell you how my father marked the walls
of his studio with the four cardinal points
and filled the rooms
with skyscapes and seascapes;
how it was years
before I knew how small the house was.
I couldn't let go,
not then: my window opened onto an aquarium
where the fins of tropical fish fluttered
like crepe. My mother's
was the mirror
at her dressing table, lit
with crystal flasks. There she sat,
while I played role after role, trying them on
as if they were dresses. When

I looked in the mirror, I saw dozens
of girls spinning there: such
shimmering choices. Petrarch imagined
an architecture of memory
where images were stored in places
of fitting size. I kept
my father's planes and my first glimpse
of the sea in a meadow
of white grass. The angry voices I heard
one New Year's Eve
in the broken pieces of ceiling
on the top floor of a warehouse.
I bent over and dropped the tea roses

I wore in my hair into night held
by the reservoir.
But that was not the end of it. When recently,

at a party, someone asked where
I'd grown up, I didn't tell him about
the fragrance of oranges in the glass garden,
the stiff silver shrubs,
the stone barge built on the edge of the bay.
I turned around and spotted you,
across the room,
staring at sycamores through the French doors.
You told me a pearl
was hidden under my tongue and, as evening emerged
from the trees in its many shapes,
I removed the pearl
and thought of how, in Japanese prints,
a girl pulls from her mouth the hair
she's stuffed there
to mute the sound of pleasure or pain.

REASONS FOR FLIGHT

As a child I squinted into the sky
and looked so hard for my father that sometimes
I felt the stars would burst from my skull
and fizzle like dropped matches on the sidewalk.
One summer he took me to the Arizona desert
where the government stored old planes,
hundreds of them in perfect, silver rows.
I looked for the spot of salt on the tail
that had grounded each one, but saw
only wind whirling sand and the ripple
of a rattlesnake under a cracked wing.
At Christmas, my teacher brought a piñata
to school; after that, I thought any plane
might explode with a dozen orange parachutes
or music tumble from the strut
and ping off the surface of the birdbath.
Later, I followed those skydivers and,
arching into the fall, promised myself always
to see the earth this way, as a kind of goal.
My father looked the other way: years before,

a recruiter had driven up to the lumberyard
in an air-conditioned car and promised the skies
were cool, the wings of jets icy to the touch,
that their black engines burned oxygen pure
as a drug. What followed was basic training,
marching miles in the dust at Lackland;
sandy runways in the Mojave; Taipei
and Wake Island and Da Nang where he stood
on the flightline and longed to chisel open
the moon and release its ancient rainwater.

71

Even as he changed the engine of a C-130
on Greenland, he felt the tools searing cold
into his hands. The Arctic sky was white:
stars barely showed at night. It occurred to him,
standing there, that extremes run in a circle
too large for us to see and that, along
the way, everything—the lines of longitude
and latitude, the woman and child waiting
on the other side of the world—had become
abstract, shimmering past all his senses.

DREAMS OF YOU COME IN PAIRS

Whoosh: the watery sound the first
or last leaves of a season make. Was that you,
saying goodbye, or simply the trees in the wind?
It was months ago. My memory of you is faulty,
like those imprecise notions of the sea
I got from the conch my uncle brought me
when I was a child. But, last night, I stood
at the French doors and watched for you
the way a gardener would watch for rain
in the century's driest summer. I expected
you to come by sea, but a car let you out
at the end of the drive and pebbles,
not bright bits of the bay, clung
to your shoes. You were dusty for days:
I wiped sand from your forehead and felt
the grit settle in my clothes.

When I woke up my arm was tired
and in the red vase on the mantel
I saw the glassblower's breath and knew that,
shaping the vase, he must have imagined
a beautiful child in a glass box,
a bitten lip. Silence is not unlike rain,
the way it falls across everything
and you watch it from somewhere you hope
is safe and warm. Later, in the country,
I saw sunflowers, larger than faces,
blooming in a field and made stone-rubbings
in an old cemetery. A light rain
darkened the pink sleeves of my shirt.

I felt at such peace, squatting there,
it was as though I'd found the grave
of a lost twin. Spoken your name. Said goodbye.

THE BOOK OF THE OCEAN TO CYNTHIA

On his first voyage here, a young Indian
had greeted him with gifts:
a parakeet, a basket of pineapples,
an armadillo. Ralegh paid them little attention,
his eye pulled inland, beyond
the Orinoco Delta. Now, as the last map
in the world entirely free
of ornament unrolled in his mind,
he imagined a parakeet
singing in the gardens of Durham House.
Bess's face in the window. A grandchild
chasing the armadillo down the stone path.
He thought of the garden where,
among metal reproductions of everything
that grew in his kingdom,
the Incan king dreamed and aged.
Gold fish, gold herbs, silver birds
in silver trees—from the deck
of the *Destiny* Ralegh listened
to the click of gold flowers
in the rain. So heavily did the ship pitch,
in the waters off Guiana, she might have been
a mammal locked in sleep, dreaming,
from her close cave, of flight.
The moon's pale footsteps climbed
the mast. His one true love.
Come closer, go away, the sea insisted;
how human it seemed to him then, the way
it made the same mistake over and over.
This was his last voyage:
neither garden was likely any longer.

The sun hissed as it set in its secret ocean
and Ralegh thought of the moon a Devonshire shepherd
would see as he climbed the hill home,
of the thousand dawns a man would witness
on his way to El Dorado where he might find
what was at once first and final.

THE CONTEMPORARY POETRY SERIES

Edited by Paul Zimmer

Dannie Abse, *One-Legged on Ice*
Gerald Barrax, *An Audience of One*
Tony Connor, *New and Selected Poems*
Franz Douskey, *Rowing Across the Dark*
Lynn Emanuel, *Hotel Fiesta*
John Engels, *Vivaldi in Early Fall*
John Engels, *Weather-Fear: New and Selected Poems, 1958–1982*
Brendan Galvin, *Atlantic Flyway*
Brendan Galvin, *Winter Oysters*
Michael Heffernan, *The Cry of Oliver Hardy*
Michael Heffernan, *To the Wreakers of Havoc*
Conrad Hilberry, *The Moon Seen as a Slice of Pineapple*
X. J. Kennedy, *Cross Ties*
Caroline Knox, *The House Party*
Gary Margolis, *The Day We Still Stand Here*
Michael Pettit, *American Light*
Bin Ramke, *White Monkeys*
J. W. Rivers, *Proud and on My Feet*
Laurie Sheck, *Amaranth*
Myra Sklarew, *The Science of Goodbyes*
Marcia Southwick, *The Night Won't Save Anyone*
Mary Swander, *Succession*
Bruce Weigl, *The Monkey Wars*
Paul Zarzyski, *The Make-Up of Ice*

THE CONTEMPORARY POETRY SERIES

Edited by Bin Ramke

J. T. Barbarese, *Under the Blue Moon*
Richard Cole, *The Glass Children*
Wayne Dodd, *Sometimes Music Rises*
Gary Margolis, *Falling Awake*
Aleda Shirley, *Chinese Architecture*
Terese Svoboda, *All Aberration*